MW01519578

BLESSINGS, TEARS
and a
CHUCKLE or TWO

BLESSINGS, TEARS
and a
CHUCKLE or TWO

(BALLADS of a WAND'RING MINSTREL)

For Sharon + Jack
May all your days be
filled with blessings + laughter
the only tears of joy!
Fondly
Willi

Willi Fischer Jed

Willi Fischer Jed
7/14

To order additional copies of this book, contact:
Xlibris Corporation
1-888-795-4274
www.Xlibris.com
Orders@Xlibris.com
86071

CONTENTS

CHRISTMAS

CHUCKLES

for Laurie, Robert, and Tim—the music of my life

for Nick and Zack—the grace notes

and in memory of my beloved Bob, the Pedal Point

BLESSINGS and TEARS

ALONE . . .

. . . she walked the silent streets
Beneath the blackness clear;
In silent snow left tiny prints—
Upon her lashes, tears.
Blindly, she trod in frozen night,
As icy crystals fell,
And frooze her in some nameless fear
She knew the numbness well.
The city streets glared patent black,
As marching sticks of light,
Deceptive danced with little taps
Beneath the waiting night.
The frozen ground beneath her feet
Spread upwards from below,
While careless winds sliced from above
Casting her in snow.
She pulled her tacky little fur
More closely round her arms,
And, shaking, slid beside a door
To hide herself from harm.
Too soon, the tired lashes closed,
And puffy clouds of breath
Slowly, like a dying leaf,
Left her, too, in death.
Warm, at last, in the Father's arm.
Free from hunger, free from harm.

BLESSING DENIED

Securely suspended
from a soft fold of the murky-red cavern,
the tiny cell floats
gently
within a cloudy tear.
A minute pulse marks time
patiently awaiting some far-off
unknown
explosion.
Sweetly it sways
in its warm moist pod,
content to let destiny
have its unremitting way.
Languidly,
it turns,
then nestles down,
having naught to do
but wait,
yet having no knowledge of what it awaits,
not even aware
of the tedium
of time passing;
it has no awareness of else.
Slowly it grows,
this changeling,
reaching hesitantly out
to probe the perimeters of its miniature cradle.
As days and night melt together,
devoid of dark or light
in this evanescent warm pool,
this wee shapeless form
so gently slumbers,
half awakens,
emits a faint throbbing heartbeat

Tiny free-form arms and legs begin to flail,
exploring,
dancing around the strange and shapeless cord
from which it draws its sustenance.
One day or night,
soft crooning sounds invade the silence:
the voice of the woman
who will one day be called
"Mother".
Already
a bond is forming
with this soothing melody.
The layers of the hazy red walls
become more taut,
as the little body grows
to fill the empty folds surrounding it.
It senses
with its whole being
the music
of what lies beyond.
It bends and stretches,
anticipating
some impending miracle.
Fleeting fragments of wonder
it cannot quite comprehend
become a part of its memory.
The little brain registers the tiny arms and legs,
pink fingers and toes
it can now move
in some semi-controlled fashion.
It smiles and dozes off
in safety and peace,
knowing that
somehow,

somewhere,
something extraordinary awaits.
Suddenly,
without warning,
a giant shining fish-scraper-like thing
violates its tiny world.
Panic!
Confusion!
A swirling vortex!
Brief agony . . .
leaving only a bloody carnage in its wake.
And a woman weeps
. . . great
. . . silent
. . . sobs.

BLESSINGS SHARED

A shimm'ring pod within the womb,
Not destined for the empty tomb;
Given life by God's decree.
Shifting, timeless as the sea,
Waiting for some velvet night
When the stars glow full and bright,
This tiny creature, graceful, free,
Birthing, fills its destiny.
The unwed mother, giving life,
Amid the pain, the stress, the strife
Give to another, a stranger, unknown,
The loving child, no longer her own.
This tiny baby, dew-kissed eyes
Gently sleeping, softly sighs;
Handed with selfless love to another,
A priceless gift, mother to mother.
Sought she not the easy way,
Honored life, the Father's way;
At Decision's Crossroads. firm did stand
And followed, in faith, her Lord's command.
Blessed, that gentle, giving one
Who sought Thy will, and it was done.
Yea, blessed be that maiden mild
Who let it live, that precious child.
Greater love could never be
That that which she has given free;
Just as the Father gave His Son,
This mother, too, did give her own.
Wipe fear and guilt and doubt away,
Tomorrow dawns a bright new day.
From future sorrow, keep her free,
And grant her peace, eternally.

ON CONFIRMATION

Today you kneel before your Lord—
He calls you by your name;
The Holy Spirit fills your heart,
The Savior finds His lamb.
This Holy Day of wond'rous joy
God's love shines brightly through,
As you, His chosen one, come forth—
Baptismal vows renew.
Welcome to God's family!
In faith and trust we pray
That you'll always feel as close to Him
As you do this special day.

ECHOES OF GOD'S CATHEDRAL

Needles softly chatter as we walk beneath the trees;
In silence do we hearken, as we fall upon our knees
In God's great, green cathedral, the sun flows dappled through-
A benison of peace within a counterpoint of blue.
A tiny cricket rubs his wings; pines hum in the breeze.
A mourning dove coos softly, awakens buzzing bees.
The birds join in, then, one by one, in full-throat harmony-
My heart chimes in quite silently, completes the symphony.
And though there be no voices, no organs, trumps, or choir,
The song of God's creation, blessing, sets the heart afire.
The forest soothes our longings, and wheresoe'er we trod,
It sets the anxious heart at ease: we are at one with God

ENDING

(With apologies to Carl Sandburg)

Death came to our house today.
It came on big
black
silent
cat feet
Langorously
patiently
It stretched itself
before the hearth.
Fearlessly
it followed me
from room to empty room.
Stealthily
it cozied near us
on our bed.
Suddenly,
its huge paw
struck down the lone rose
on my nightstand.
The crash
covered the sound
of my heart
as they shattered
simultaneously.
You have been on intimate terms
with the cat;
I just met him.
Death came to our house today.

It came on big
black
silent
cat
feet.
Langorously
patiently
it stretched itself out
before the hearth.
You let him in.

FOOTSTEPS

Countless footsteps wend their ways,
with each awakening dawn,
And where they walk, their imprints echo,
long past set of sun.
Silent hearts beat cadence
as they're helpless borne along,
Mingled with each other
in a suppliant, whispered song.
The choir, a pedal point of life,
of seeking . . . sorrow . . . need . . .
If one should only listen,
one would find a soul to feed.
Within cacophony, Oh, Lord,
keep me attuned, I pray;
Let my song touch with love, those lives
I pass along the way.

FRIENDSHIP . . .

. . . is a garden
Grown from friendly deeds,
Planted in another's heart,
Growing memories.
Fragrant blossoms bloom and grow
In blessings without end;
I thank my God each day for you;
I love you, dearest friend!

HE IS NOT GONE

Think on me with mem'ries sweet;
I am not gone, nor do I sleep;
Naught but an empty shell lies here:
I am in the arms of my Saviour dear.
Surounded in His radient grace,
Behold my Saviour face to face.
Kneeling at the Father's throne,
Rejoice! I've found the pathway home.
Peace surrounds me, more serene
Than ever dreamt in earthly dream.
A mighty organ sounds on high,
And trumpets echo through the sky.
He bids me join His angel choir,
Where earthly song could ne'er aspire.
Those gone ahead, once more I meet;
In tears of joy, my loved ones greet.
Thus, sorrow not; sing out in joy!
Loved ones, I am ever nigh.
And look to the day when again we'll meet
Glorified, at Jesus' feet.

TOGETHER FOREVER

Although my Saviour's called me Home.
You'll never ever be alone
When you sing a joyful song,
Hear my soft carol sing along.
When the wind sweeps through the trees,
My voice is singing on the breeze.
When stars shine out in velvet night,
I'm smiling down in bright star's light.
When snowflakes fall upon your cheek,
It's my tiny kiss so soft and meek.
When you hear a baby cry,
The tiny tear falls from my eye.
In midst of a children's joyful play,
My laughter's never far away.
You'll see me in the sunset's ray,
God's benedicion on the day.
And if a rainbow you should spy,
Know I ride the blue one by.
When you turn sweet soil in Spring,
The daisy's smile, my smile will bring.
When you hear sweet choirs sing,
Know I'm near you, listening.
By day or night, my watch I'll keep
Come to you in dreams so sweet,
Our dearest Saviour, our glorious guide,
We'll walk together by your side.
God bless and keep you, loved one sweet,
Till we meet again at Jesus feet.

THE GIFT OF SONG

Once angels had no voices, for what had they to say?
Enough they guarded over all God's creatures day by day.
Once there were no angel choirs, for what had they to do,
But make a proclamation to a holy man or two.
Swift and bright and joyful, went about their daily deeds,
Looking o'er the Father's flock, supplying daily needs,
Until that blessed day of days when Jesus came to earth.
And all the angels gathered to proclaim His blessed birth.
They echoed from the mountain tops, heraldic voices raised
In glorious Alleluias, as the new-born King they praised.
Still now, we hear the angels in a mother's lullaby,
Or in the sweet, fresh laughter of a little girl or boy;
We hear them in the chuckle of the stranger on the street;
We hear them in the greeting of each dear new friend we meet;
We hear them in the chapel, as in love we join the throng
To thank Thee, Father, bless Thee for the glorious gift of song.

HANDS

We walk a busy, hectic path
From dawn to set of sun,
Engaged in countless little tasks
That surely must be done;
But this is the wish I always wish,
The prayer I always pray:
Lord, may my life help other lives
It touches on the way.

WITH JESUS, WALK

Music lingers in the memory,
Persists within the mind,
To keep the weary soul at peace
In a world that's less than kind.
The simple phrase of a well-loved hymn
Persists throughout the day;
Perhaps God's greatest gift to us,
When too weary are we to pray.
Each measured step on the steep, hard road
Is accompanied by a song;
Learned as a child, God's promises sing
Within, as we go along:
"And He walks with me,
and He talks with me,
And He tells me I am His own,
And the joys we share
as we tarry there
None other has ever known."

IN THE BEGINNING . . .

. . . was The Word
And it was given to man,
And then, the Father gave us voice
To worship in His plan;
And it was good that man had voice
And God it did delight
That man could offer words of prayer
Yet something seemed not right.
Then angels winged to earth one day
And the Spirit came along,
And they all came near to bless us
With the joyous gift of song.
Then humankind as one could join
And grateful voices raise,
And as the angels choirs on high,
They, too, could sing their praise.
And music sweet enhanced The Word,
And the gift that God hath sent
Filled the heart and soul with love
In sounds magnificent.
To speak with God brings comfort,
But when souls unite in song,
The air resounds in echoes of love
From the mighty blessed throng.

LIFE'S JOURNEY . . .

. . . is not merely the process
of putting one foot before the other
on some well-worn road . . .
Rather,
it's the joyful song
of the climber
who ascends the
lofty mountain heights . . .
The sweet melody
that sings to the dreamer
in the valley . . .
The pure pleasure
of knowing
some new and magical path
thus far not taken.

MARIA

God could not be everywhere,
So He created mothers fair:
He took the strength of the stately pine,
The smile of the rippling brook;
From a star, He took the glow,
From an angel, the radiant look
Caring, loving, warmth, and joy,
He lavished freely on,
Then added a sense of humor
And came up with—my mom

DANCING ON THE EDGE

(Echoes of a Mental Colony)

The maze is a people-mover in a box.
It lacks top or bottom—Is girded only by highs and lows
Empty-eyed, stooped shadows
Are slowly transported from corner to endless corner
Round and round.
In some grotesque funereal dirge of despair,
They trudge on.
Heavy legs shuffle ever so slightly
Under bowed heads. So slowly the clones tread,
One would question there being any movement. At all.
At regular intervals,
All motion ceases briefly
As the chemical mind-petrol is refilled.
And the box becomes all.
And the fear becomes that the maze might end
And one might fall off the end
There to float endlessly
Like some distant astronaut
Flung free from his tether.
Occasionally the vacuum of silence is broken
By a frantic scream, A smothered sob.
As hearts shatter
Like Goblets
In a silent movie.
Yet hope comes in the form of a Small,
Tenuous,
Featherling
Kiss.

SERENDIPITY

The mind it is a shining place
Alight with beauty, style and grace;
A glist'ning pool of flowing streams,
Of glowing,softly falling dreams.

The mind it is a sparkling thing,
A flashing, flaming, hidden ring—
A crash of thunder, rush of rain,
Cloudburst, exploding, ignite the brain.

The mind it is a will-o-the-wisp
Where earthly bound'ries cease to exist;
Whimsies of wonder fly to and fro,
And, far too oft, forgotten go.

The mind—ah! if we might recall
The phantoms passing through it all!
The magic kaleidoscope I might be
If all those mirages remained with me!

FOR MY SPECIAL MOM AND DAD

In my heart, there lives a little song
Which I would sing for you;
It tells about my Father's world
And all that He can do.
He made the sun, He makes the rain,
He makes the flowers to grow;
He made the moon that silver shines,
The sparkling stars that glow.
He gave us life, he gives us food,
And I'm especially glad
He gives me everything I need
In my loving Mom and Dad.

MY DEAREST FRIEND . . .

. . . though you and I
Are many miles apart,
I carry loving thoughts of you
E'er constant in my heart.
The joyous, laughing times we've shared
Throughout these many years—
The sorrows, cares, and stormy days
Worn smooth by loving tears;
The prayers we offered quietly,
As hands we'd tightly hold.
The friendship that you offered me,
More precious far than gold;
We spoke in glances, silent,
As our thoughts transcended speech:
My mirror image in my heart
Where I can always reach.
You dwell with me in constant love
Which miles can ne'er erase,
But, oh what joy 'twould bring to me
To see your smiling face.

FRIENDSHIP

The gift of song, you've shared with me,
The gift of love,—you've cared with me,
New beginnings you've dared with me,
Whatever came, been there for me.
In times of woe, spoke prayer with me.
Greater inspiration, no one e'er could be;
You'll never know what a blessing you've been—
I thank my *God* for you, my friend.

NIGHT IN THE BARRIO

Silver moon slips silently
over shifting shadows.
The torrid dessert day is no more
And only blood
now hotly pulses.
The soft syllibant strains
of a hushed guitar
strum softly
As young lovers steal off
to secret places
To intimate places
Fondling, Caressing.

A grizzled old man sits
on a square stucco step
milking a bottle of clear liquid;

Somewhere
a tiny baby cries
And permeating all,
the hot breath
and acrid sweet smell
of sex
lights its own fire.

HOME WITH JESUS

Though you see him not, he's only flown
To a wondrous, new celestial home
He lies not buried in the ground,
By earthly ties no longer bound.
Stand not o'er his grave and weep,
He is not here, nor doth he sleep.
Two beauteous angels, shining bright,
Came and led him toward the light.
He felt no fear, was wont to go,
Unfettered, freed from chains below.
Gone the sorrows, grief, and pain,
To a place where love and peace do reign.
It matters not how poor nor grand
His life here on this earthly plain;
Now riches and joy beyond compare
Surround his being everywhere.
He beholds, anon, his mother's face;
Again he feels her warm embrace;
His father, too, comes to enfold
That loving child he once did hold.
And friends of old stand all about;
Bid him welcome, seek him out,
In health and bliss and youth replete,
With open arms. the loved ones greet.
The light enhanced, it seems unreal,
Gently falls in grace to kneel,
For, before him, on His glorious throne,
Pierced hands reach out to bring him home
What rapture fills him as he sighs
And meets his Saviour's gentle eyes.
So do not mourn, he is not gone,
You'll never, ever walk alone.
His spirit walks and talks with you,
Through pain and pleasure, guides you through.
Until that blessed day you'll meet
Face to face at Jesus' feet

REQUIEM

Like idle thoughts,
Snow drifts Gently
down To kiss the earth.

In seemingly fanciful flight,
my Soul Slips silently
Following the Silvery White Lace

Spinning
Spinning
Awaiting a promise shared.

Heedlessly
Carelessly
The Soul descends,

Realizing, Too late,
that Cold Ground
was meant for Icy Snow

And the Soul's
True Purpose
lies in its Ascent.

SONNETS 3

IN _ FORM _ ELIZABETHAN
Even as the sun spills liquid gold
A vaulted veil of conquest smoth'ring night,
So springs my ever anxious heart, behold:
Subservient humble-bowed within thy light.
As barren earth sucks up each droplet dear
Of dew, before by temporal fire devoured,
So drink I from thy black eyes clear, as though
To drain my cup before anew 'tis poured.
As breezes gently play upon Pan's Pipes
And set to life ripe, swaying choirs of trees,
So bend I, yielding, suppliant in thy sight
With eagerness, my love, to serve and please.
        And yet. when twilight lenses filter sun,
        'Tis love alone, requited, makes us one

IN _ FORM _ PETRARCHAN
Be joy and love mere words professed
From loving lip to anxious ear,
A whispered word to still the fear
Arising, unbid, in silent behest?
Could love dwell in, unwelcomed guest,
Demanding entry, denying reproof?
Love sole doth thrive where Truth
Lays lovers unified in rest.
        In tragedy, in shrieking birth;
        Close bound are they in labours shared;
        Limbs entwined by quiet hearth
        Where flame or fading cinders flared.
        In thy black eyes, I seek my worth;
        Our souls in joyous union paired.

IN _ FORM _ ALL
Beneath my bonnet lives no sonnet,
Though, heav'n knows I'll try to slip something by—
Metaphors piled like clouds in the sky—
Success is as distant as last year's comet;
My poor bumbling brain just cannot get on it!
It's not just my writing of sonnets, 'tis clear,
That dubiously labels me, 'sonneteer'.
A sonnet! A sonnet! Can't write one, doggonit!
(Iambic pentameter—I'll never get that)
As I stand here in awe of the writers of oc-taves—
Of the Shakespeares and Wordsworths and Browning conclaves,
"tcould surely be said, 'They knew where 'twas at!'
          Though my fancy lies buried deep back in Baroque,
          I'm stuck in the era of Pepsi and Coke

STEEL

God's promise, as written in The Book,
If we come to Him in prayer:
He'll never leave us comfortless,
Give us more than we can bear,
The hotter the fire, the more tempered the steel;
He molds us in His will.
He let's "old Satan" do his best
That we'll be stronger still.
(Sometimes, though, one might ponder
The reason for all these "favors"—
And, might it occur to Him sometimes
To strengthen, perhaps, one's neighbor?)

TEARS . . .

. . . like Tiny Diamonds
Roll slowly down
Easily as costly,
They are purchased with Pain
and Loss
They are formed by
the Fire of the Soul
They are the Issue
of the Searching Mind.
Tears:
Gently
Kindly
Kiss alabaster Cheeks
Cleansing
Caressing
Forgiving
Laying wide the
Hidden Pathway
to the Heart
Leaving it Vulnerable
and Open
to God's Healing Grace.

THE GARDNER

Slowly, the bud unfolds its wings,
One petal at a time,
Until a brilliant bloom explodes,
And. beauteous, makes it's climb.
    The perfect flower stands tall in grace,
    Its glory fills my eyes,
    Until, one day, the graceful head
    Hangs slowly down and dies.
I turn it deep in fertile ground,
As sorrow clouds my eyes,
Yet, I know that life will come again:
The rose again shall rise.
    And as I kneel and till my soil,
    I think on greater loss:
    I see my blessed Saviour
    As He hangs upon the cross.
I see His blessed head hang down;
I see Him slowly die;
I see His bleeding hands and feet—
"It is finished", His final sigh.
    I see my Jesus laid to rest;
    In borrowed tomb He lies.
    Then radiance fills my every being
    As I see my Lord arise.
I know, one day, I'll be the rose,
Body in earth laid down,
And my soul shall ascend to my King's own home,
My bloom, my heavenly crown.

WINTER'S BLOSSOMS

The years since childhood danced and marched
Midst boasts and songs and cheers;
And friendships came and went—or grew—
Midst chatter, smiles, and tears.
Companions of youth, now mostly spent
And lost along the way;
Those to whom we pledged our hearts,
Faded with yesterday.
A few there are who yet do bloom
Within the small bouquet,
Yet, when a beauteous new friend does gleam,
'Tis a rich and glittering ray.
A wond'rous gift in seasoned years,
This dear and loving friend,
With whom to share and love and laugh;
A blessing without end.
I'm grateful for your warmth and charm,
The grace in all you do;
And, most of all, my dearest Friend,
Thanks for being you!

Christmas

THE ANGEL

The Babe in the manger radiated a light
That outshown the star on high
Shepherds and Magi knelt as one;
She hovered closer by.
All fear had fled as she ventured near,
Drawn by that Blessed Child;
This must be the Jesus, the long fortold,
Who'd one day be defiled.
To rest, she settled atop the shed
Where the Holy One did lie.
You will see her still and evermore
On each creche at Chrismas tide.
Carry us all to Bethlehem
That, in glory, we may see
What God hath sent to earth that night,
Our Saviour for to be.
My wish for you is that, like that angel,
Blessed by the Holy Son,
In love and faith, in hope and joy,
We, too, may closer come.

A blessed year, good health, dear friends
Simple wishes we send.
Strike the harp! Alleluias sing!
Gloryify our New-born King!

ODE TO JOY

Strike the harp and sound the horn—
Jesus, the Prince of Peace, is born.
Why, then, no great symphony
Of trump and drum to welcome Thee?
    From the rooftops, shout the cry:
    The Son of God, our King, is nigh!
    Yet, Mary simply sighs in awe;
    The only music, shifting straw
Whereon the New-born Babe doth sleep,
And barnyard creatures vigil keep.
When from the navy velvet sky.
A brilliant star explodes on high,
    Beams upon a bleating lamb
    Who stirs the silent Bethlehem.
    A gentle cow doth softly low;
    The cock, alert, begins to crow.
Shepherds waken, dumb with fear,
As glistening silver rays draw near,
And midst these lights begin to sing
Herald angels for their King.
    Thus, let us all with heart and voice
    With radiant heavenly hosts rejoice,
    And let us now and ever be
    Christ's ever-praising symphony.

THE SECOND TIME AROUND

Our Saviour's birth draws ever near
Midst songs of angels—do you hear?
Bells ring out in dark nights clear,
And man awaits the blest New Year.

We've suffered loss of loved ones new
Shed tears of joy and and sorrows, too,
Through clouds may loom, we look to you
Where skies still shimmer, ever blue.

Again, we seek the Holy Child
And know that He is ever nigh,
And hearts are gladdened, spirits fly;
No time for grief, no time to sigh.

Trumpets sound throughout the earth,
And hearts are gladdened by His birth
Love will swell in blessed mirth,
Behold the future, seek it's worth.

This Tiny Babe, knows He His plight—
From cross and death to glorious light,
To save us from this earthly night
And take us home to beauty bright?

And midst the bells and trump and song,
We seek His path and walk along,
And fear and longing—all are gone
As we await our heav'nly crown.

No worthy gift to give this Child,
We men, who are by sin defiled,
Need only believe in His mercy mild
And follow Him, by Grace beguiled.

CHRISTMAS AT OUR HOUSE

Christmas at our house, most precious of times—
The voices of carolers, the ringing of chimes;
The candle-lit worship we share at the church
To hear the sweet story of Jesus's birth;
The log on the hearth, crackling in joy,
The anticipation of each girl and boy;
The crunch of the footsteps on fresh-fallen snow.
Beneath soft dark night, where the twinkling stars glow,
As the relatives come bearing gifts and good wishes,
And Mom can be heard setting out the best dishes.
The turkey is served up, all toasty and brown,
And cranberries and pie, 'til no more will go down.
The little ones anxiously peer at the tree
Wond'ring, "Which of those presents is meant just for me?"
Parcels soon opened and chaos does reign—
Ribbons and wrappers, one lone candy cane.
After a while, the little ones doze,
Chubby arms curled 'round some toy in a pose.
Dad lifts them gently and puts them to bed,
Laying a kiss on each damp little head.
Grandma and Grandpa exchange a soft smile,
Reminded of days long ago for a while.
Full up to bursting with joy and goodwill,
We quietly chat in the nighttime so still.
The Yule log turns gently to embers aglow,
And outside the windows, the falling of snow
Makes us realize, that, whatever ever else may be,
Christmas is family and always will be.
As the Father of all sent His own Precious Son
To bless us and teach us and make us all one.
To our brothers and sisters, our love we would send,
And His hope, joy. and peace, and life without end.

TREES AND DREDELS

It's time for chimes and bells that ring;
It's time for snow and happy things,
For silent, star-filled velvet nights,
For candles and cookies and hidden delights.

This cherished season brings special days
Of warmth and joy and hope and praise,
Of love to last the whole year through,
Of happy thoughts of friends like you.

MARY'S LULLABY

As angels sound their trumps on high—
-The Virgin croons a lullaby-
Horns peal forth in joyous mirth
To tell the news of Jesus' birth;
Shepherds wake to dance and sing
And make their way to Bethlehem
Where in the manger Jesus lies-
-And Mary croons a lullaby-
Harp and lute call near and far,
And heaven boasts a brilliant star
To lead Three Kings who now process
Across the desert wilderness
To bring their gifts of treasures rare
To lay before the Royal Heir;
The world breaks forth in songs of joy-
-While Mother croons her lullaby-
Angels, Wise Men, shepherds, star;
Music ringing near and far,
Resounding in the blazing sky-
-The Virgin sings soft lullaby-
Let us rejoice and dance and sing
Our songs of praise to Christ our King,
But in our hearts, keep ever nigh,
-That sweet, soft, loving lullaby.

THE REASON FOR THE SEASON

It was a black and velvet night
When, suddenly, there shone a light
Which lit the very earth below,
And all mankind beheld the glow,
Golden trumpets rhapsodized
From out those crystal star-filled skies.

A blinding array of golden flame
As heavenly Alleluias rang
In praise to Christ, the new-born King;
The Glorias o'er the hills did ring.
Hillside shepherds, tending sheep,
Wakened from their fitful sleep.

The rich, the lame, the halt, the poor,
Beheld the ray, set forth to adore.
What Child was this? What drew them on,
As morning softly followed dawn?
It was Messiah, prophesied,
An age-old promise satisfied.

And all went forth to find this King;
But why led the star to Bethlehem?
A homely village of humble folk—
Was this, then, some ironic joke?
No palace stood within the town,
But graceless homes of no renown.

Three wise men journeyed from afar
Followed, in awe, that brilliant star.
To a stable poor behind an inn
(No lodging was to be had therein)
And, as they approached so breathlessly,
They looked within, fell to the knee;

For lying there, midst straw and hay,
A tiny beauteous Infant lay,
Surrounded by cow and ass and sheep,
As the carpenter, Joseph, watch did keep,
The blessed Virgin gently sighed
And welcomed guests as they arrived.

Did He know, e'en then, that radiant Child,
Now lying in manger, meek and mild,
That, one day, for the likes of you and like I,
He must, alone, go forth to die?
Did He know, e'en then, He was God's own Son
Made Man, Sacrifice, for us to become?

Perhaps, He always knew, and yet,
He walked His path without regret.
Let us never forget, this blessed season,
That, without Calvary, there is no reason
To celebrate now and joyfully sing
The coming of Christmas, of Christ the King.

Let us sing, with joy, the angels' song;
In trust and faith, steadfast and strong;
Let us vow, once again, to love a bit more,
To be kinder, more caring, more like Him, than before.
If this Spirit of Christmas we keep through the year,
Then the reason for the season will always be clear.

This, then, is my wish for you, dearest friend:
That the blessing of Christmas for you never ends
That on life's darkest nights, that bright shining star
Guide your path with its light, wherever you are.
God bless you and keep you all safe from harm
And hold you e'er close in His Loving Arms.

THE SECOND TIME AROUND

A silken night, a star shines bright,
The world in slumber lies.
While softly croons, 'neath silver moon,
A Mother's lullabye.

In stable hushed, midst straw and rush,
A tiny Babe does sleep,
And dozing nigh on hillsides high,
Young shepherds watch do keep.

From lands afar, led by that star,
Three Wise Men riches bring;
No maps they hold, but men of old
Told stories of a King.

A flash! The night is set alight,
As Heav'nly herald throngs,
Split the air with anthems fair,
Triumph in their songs.

The mewling bleat of awakened sheep
Accompanies the sound,
As shepherds wake and fairly quake
In awe of angels 'round.

They hasten there to stable bare,
Not doubting what they see:
This Child who lay in manger hay
The Son of God must be.

Were herders sure, this Infant pure
Was Messiah, long foretold?
Did they not gaze in morning's haze
Our Savior to behold?

Did not each King his treasure bring,
Bow lowly to the ground
In adoration, no hesitation,
Riches spread around?

Should star appear in the eastern sphere
Would we so faithful climb?
Would we believe, this Child receive,
Or simply, not have time?

If there walked around our busy town
An earnest, pleading Man,
Invite us to dine at His table of wine,
Would we quickly reply, "I can"?

Would we skip that brunch, that business lunch,
That game of golf at tee,
To follow a sight whose clothes "weren't right"
Just because He said, "Follow me"?

Would it make much sense to follow hence
Wherever He might lead?
Would we summon our friends, take our children's hands,
And earnestly pay Him heed?

Or would we be sad, yet call Him mad —
Hang Him from symbolic tree;
Would we Him spurn, or choose to learn,
Receive Him, joyously?

The Son of Man shall come again—
Be watchful, that ye see;
We all shall meet at Jesus' feet
And at the Father's knee.

And, again, the night will be set alight,
And we'll join that heav'nly throng
Who fill the air with music rare,
Triumphant in our song.

May a glad Noel within you dwell,
And hope and health and cheer,
And follow, dear friend, that Christ, without end
Through a blessed joy-filled year.

CHRISMAS ALL YEAR

When we bend to help a little child,
When we dry another's tears;
When we aid the old and lonely
And chase away their fears;
When we listen to a neighbor
Or lend a helping hand,
When we welcome every challenge
And strive to understand;
See brothers and sisters clearly
Without color, race, or creed;
When we know that all in living
Is the simple, honest deed;
Then we can say we've made it;
We've given love and cheer—
We're living the spirit of Christmas
Each day throughout the year.

THE THREE MARYS

I want to be with Jesus
As He hangs upon the cross;
To weep with Mother Mary
Know her sorrow, touch her loss.
To feel the earth's great wrenching cry,
As tar-streaked heavens are rent.
I want, in Death, to prostrate lie
With Him; my last breath spent.
I want to walk with Mary
And with Mary Magdalene,
Bearing oils and linens fine-
Then—struck dumb, as in some dream.
For, from Joseph's tomb, there shown a light
More brilliant than the sun;
"He is not here, He's risen!"
Spoke an angel of the Son.
No angel, I; I'm lowly, weak,
Though I'd gladly ope'd the tomb;
Just to have been a Mary—
Stand in radiance in that room.
We each have our own Calvery,
Each bear some heavy cross,
Have suffered, hurt, lost some one dear;
And known that sense of loss.

Yet, when I go to my Calv'ry
To feel my earthly pain,
To feel alone on my Golgatha,
Think on my Saviour, slain.
I think on Mother Mary,
And on Mary Magdalene,
Our tears are blending, flowing free,
For Salvation have we seen!

THE HOLY CHILD'S TREE

Once there was a little tree,
Grew in the others' shade—
Crooked, lonesome, angular,
Rough and sadly frayed.
The woodsman saw it there one day,
Just shook his head and glanced;
He walked on by another to seek,
One grand, of regal stance.
The snow fell down in feathered flakes,
Covered the tiny tree;
The sunlight danced and sparked there
In beauty none could see
Until the woodsman's Child came by
And looked upon the sight;
He hung the limbs with seeds and nuts,
God's creature to delight.
May we each see the other through
The eyes of that innocent Child;
Then will we truly see His Son,
The Jesus, meek and mild.

YULETIDE

Spring is the season of freshness and green,
Summer, the season of sun;
Fall is the season of gold and bronze,
Christmas is all these in one.
Freshness, we find in the holly and pine;
Sun, we behold in His grace;
Gold is the the friendship we feel all around,
As warmth spreads from place to place.
The season of Yule possesses these all
Encompassing all of the year—
So hold each day close with your love, dearest friends,
And greet each new season with cheer.

Chuckles

THE CHERUB CHOIR

The Cherub Choir is aptly named,
Angels small it encloses;
Some look 'round for Mom and Dad,
Some swipe at runny noses.
Some come dressed in little suits,
Some in frills and laces;
Some are clad in overalls,
Some wear dirty faces.
Some are slightly ill at ease,
Some wriggle in their sneakers,
And, always there's that little guy
Who'll never require speakers.
Some are toothless, some well scrubbed;
Some know all the words,
While others look about in fright
Like tiny newborn birds.
But, whatever they sing, however they sound,
Midst scratching, smiles and sneezes,
Somehow, I'm certain, their precious songs
Our dear Lord more than pleases.

EXERCISE CLASS AT THE "Y"—WHY?

I've done the health club, spa, and "Y" . . .
And why? I have no good reply.
Ladies in various sizes and shapes
Gyrate and writhe and strut like apes.
Some are slim—why are they there—
To prove that fate is less than fair?
With furtive glance, I hope to see
Some ill-shaped bod more rotund than me.
My eyes grow round, I shamelessly stare
At a sylph-like creature with flowing hair.
No matter how I stretch and jump,
My body still is mostly plump.
My sweats are black and understated
In hopes my rear won't be debated;
Amidst the spandex pink and puce,
My boobs hide out in XL loose.
Endless hours of perspiration,
Mind and soul in consternation,
With grim grin plastered on my lips,
I battle bulges on my hips;
I punish calves and arms and thighs,
I work! Let no one note my size.
My body, I will pound and build
Into something muscle-filled.
I'll drip on till my size ten fits!
Oh, what's the use; this is the pits!
I guess I might as well go home . . .
Right after I stop for that ice cream cone.

FANCY'S FLIGHT

Something awoke me, one summer's day
And, barefoot, I ran to see;
I looked about and scratched my head,
Saw nothing but my tree.

My footprints followed me around
The grass beneath my willow;
I settled down amongst its roots,
Head on arms did pillow.

I spied some busy ants at work,
All marching in a row,
Carrying tiny bits of food
Beneath the earth to stow.

The day grew warm, a golden day,
As a bumbly buzzy bee
Kissed the daisy near my cheek,
Which politely bowed to me.

I blinked my eyes, then looked about,
Where the velvet blue-white face
Of a nearby pansy smiled at me
With a shy and gentle grace.

The blades of grass beneath my head
Tickled at my cheek,
As a new-born breeze began to play
A game of hide and seek.

I've always longed to ride the breeze
Across the summer sky,
To fly with happy dancing leaves
And fluff the clouds near by.

I'd dip and sway from place to place,
Perhaps I'd get a peek
Of a feathery chickadee feeding her chicks
Who in soft nest did peep.

From a limb, a 'pillar winks at me
From out his fuzzy face;
A flutterbye waves her lovely wing,
Like some fluted, colorful lace.

A sudden gust sweeps me higher still,
Twirling me around;
As I spin and laugh and somersault
So high above the ground.

I spread my arms as wide as far,
I clear a chimney top;
I stop a moment, looking down—
It's a very scary drop.

Should I go hurtling to the earth
And fall, quite out of control,
There'd be nothing left but a blob of me
On the ground, in a little hole.

But, now, that's silly! I can fly!
A free and swooping kite,
And I dip and climb like a shiny plane,
My wings stretched out in flight.

Higher and higher, now I go,
Up through the atmosphere;
Is that my house I spy below?
Too tiny to be clear!

The sun shines brightly, warming me,
The breeze begins to slow,
I find I'm drifting back to earth;
I do not want to go.

But all good things must end, they say,
And, my head still soft on God's pillow,
I stretch and rub my sleepy eyes,
And look up to see my willow.

I lie in the grass and it tickles my knees;
Was my journey some dreamy flight?
Or did I really sweep and soar
Across the heavens so bright?

It really doesn't matter, you know,
'Cause whenever I want to, I may
Lie on the grass and close my eyes
Until I drift away.

GNUS FROM THE ZOOS

One day a gnu from the local zoo
Decided to travel to Timbuktu.
He was handsome and lean and slightly green,
And on this trip was very keen!
He hung his pack upon his back
To carry along on the well-worn track.
He had to bring so many things
From toothbrush to P.J.s to ropes tied in rings.
His drum and his horn—and an ear of corn
To snack on for breakfast the following morn.
He waved goodbye to his wifey pie
And told her he'd be back bye and bye.
He didn't wait, but closed the gate,
And quickly set off lest it get too late.
He climbed the trees; he swam the seas;
He soon became tired from his nose to his knees.
But he wasn't sad, he was truly glad,
Loving the wonderful times that he had.
Then, one fine day, many months away,
He found Timbuktu, but he didn't stay.
He was homesick, you know, and he started to go
Back to his home where they loved him so.
He was overjoyed, too, as he reached the zoo,
As his wifey said, "Dear, I've got gnus for you!"

MEN OF STEEL

God's promise, as written in The Book,
If we come to Him in prayer:
He'll never leave us comfortless,
Give us more than we can bear,
The hotter the fire, the more tempered the steel;
He molds us in His will.
He let's "old Satan" do his best
That we'll be stronger still.
(Sometimes, though, one might ponder)
The reason for all these "favors"—
And, might it occur to Him sometimes
To strengthen, perhaps, one's neighbor?

GRANDMA AND GRAMPS

Grandpa has a fishing pole,
He lets you fish from off his boat:
He swims about the lake with you,
And teaches you to safely float.

Now, Grandma has a cookie jar
Filled up with chewy chocolate chips;
Sometimes she even lets you help,
And, from the beaters. lick the bits.

When there's something special you *really* want,
It's hard to know—though it's apparent:
Whatever it is you'd like to have,
Either one would say yes before a parent.

GRANDPA, YOUR MUSTACHE BROKE OFF TODAY!

Grandpa, your mustache broke off today—
While I was sleeping, it went away;
How did it happen? I cannot say,
But, Grandpa, your mustache broke off today.

Grandpa, your mustache broke off today;
Is your face cold since it's gone away?
Your smile looks so strange; do I like it that way,
Since, Grandpa, your mustache broke off today?

Grandpa, your mustache broke off today;
Your lip feels all smooth where my fingers play;
Your kisses don't tickle my nose this way;
Oh, Grandpa, your mustache broke off today!

Grandpa, your mustache broke off today;
One thing makes me worried, I have to say:
Are you still the same Grandpa who loves me all day,
Now that your mustache broke off today?

You say it's *not* broken—you *shaved* it away?
That's *silly!* Let's just go outdoors now and play,
Then your lip will get darker and match you okay,
And no one will notice it broke off today.

HIGH TOPS

If my old shoe could talk to me,
I wonder if he'd balk at me
About the miles he's had to run
On hot streets, steaming in the sun.
Does he like getting slick and cool,
Skipping through some muddy pool?
Does he get squeamish, big bad feller,
While squashing some fat caterpillar?
Does he at times wish to recant
For stepping on some wayward ant?
Does he have feelings, then, as well
As to the way my feet might smell?
Is he quite friendly with his laces
Holding together his grimy places?
Is he proud of the colorful sticky toll
Of all the gum balls stuck to his sole
Does he take pride in the real neat peel
Of rubber wearing off his heel?
If my old shoe were somewhat new,
Would he even have a clue
Of how to pedal on my bike
So I could ride on, no hands, like?
Could he kick a can, a rock, a ball,
If he weren't who he was at all?
I think he likes his life just so;
He *is* my shoe, so I should *know!*
Please, Mom, no washer—don't you see?
We'd *both* lose our identity!

TREES

I like to lie beneath the trees
From Spring to golden Fall:
Some er' lacy,
Some er' tall;
Some er' swayin' over all.

I like to watch the shining leaves
From Spring to golden Fall:
Some er' yellow,
Some er' green;
Some er' Summer in between.

I like to dance beneath the trees
From Fall to sparkling Winter:
Their arms I use
For snowmen white
Till new Spring leaves grow green and bright.

IN THE VERNACULAR

I've not the new freedom
of impassioned youth—
Things are now quite insipid
I spoke in "uncouth".

Le DIET—Le's TRYIT

It seems no matter where I'm at,
The conversation turns to fat
And diet pills and calories;
Pass another cookie, please!

THE JOGGER

He-males, she-males, bounding past—
Lord, what makes you run so fast?
Is there some perverted fun
In ending up where you begun?

HO HUM . . .

Note the happy twilight jogger,
Nose in air and knees raised high . . .
How I envy his persuasion
From the chaise whereon I lie.

THE GOLFER

The golfer hides behind his tee,
In hopes that no one else may see
Unless that erudite son-of-a-gun
Should make a righteous hole in one.

THE TEENSY MAN WHO WASN'T THERE

I know a creature wee and small
Who lives by the bannister in the hall.
He spends his spare time sliding down,
Then climbs back up, a tipsy clown.
He wanders 'round when no one's home,
Making toll calls on the phone.
He leaves his hand prints on the wall,
And I get blamed, cuz, after all,
Adults can't see imaginary creatures
Or even picture their mean little features.
He drops my bath towels on the floor,
And spills my milk, and slams the door.
He rudely shouts outdoors at play,
He breaks the eggs the chickens lay.
He pulls the tail of the neighbor's dog,
And pokes a stick at the rear of my frog.
He crudely burps for hours and hours;
He spits on the sidewalks and tramples the flowers.

And you know what makes me maddest of all?
Mom doesn't believe there's a man in the hall!

MIDDLE-AGED DOLLS

If I could be your Santa Claus,
My suffering sisters in menopause,
I'd dump these valued gifts at your door . . .
Gifts you have lost that you cherished of yore.

I'd deliver to you all that maidenly vigor
That goes right along with a wee size-eight figure,
I'd restore all the color that once graced your hair
Before rinses and bleaches took residence there.

I'd bring back the contours with which youth is gifted,
So that things now suspended need not be uplifted;
I'd draw in those stomachs and soothe down those backs,
Till you'd be a dream, walking, in bun-hugging slacks.

I'd remove all the wrinkles—leave only one chin,
So you needn't spend hours rubbing grease on your skin.
You wouldn't have flashes or queer dizzy spells;
You wouldn't hear noises or ringing of bells.

No searching the closets to find the right clothes,
No hunting for spectacles right on your nose;
No shots in the arm or the hip or the fanny
By a doctor who thinks you're a nervous old granny.

No remembering that book titled, "all passion spent',
And asking yourself where the heck passion went;
No ignoring your man when he tries to contrive
To talk to that chick in channel number five.

Yes, if I were old Santa, these things I'd deliver:
The romance of cupid with his little quiver,
A lift of the heart when the valves start to whistle,
The joys of the spirit as light as a thistle.

But, alas, I'm not Santa; I'm just simply me,
The matronliest matron you ever did see;
I wish I were there sharing symptoms I've got,
But I'm due at Doc Seizures right now for a shot!

ODE TO EMACIATION

Here's to the days to us soon lost;
Here's to the many fat bucks it'll cost.
Here's to the fudge and the choc'lit chips;
Here's to the ice cream and ample hips.

Here's to rich whipped cream—one extra dab.
Here's to the tummies, the fannies, the flab;
Here's to the busoms that touch the toes;
Here's to the four-siz-ed closets of clothes.

Here's to the end of our ample proportions;
Here's to the last of those second portions.
Here's to the end of those lives of sin;
Here's to where we're going, to where we've been!

Methinks the roaring hippopotomus
Doth have a most enormous glottomus;
From him, one may see just what will happen
If the mouth of the creature be always snappin'.

Here's to the lot of us, svelte and slim;
We'll brave the suit, get in the swim;
We'll give up food, we'll lose the fat;
We'll only have bones where once we sat.

The jackets, the tunics, all, we'll shed;
Passing men, we'll spin their heads;
We'll beat them off with chain and looks
Need chastity belts with extra hooks.

We'll live, we'll laugh, we'll dance, we'll spin;
We'll die of hunger, but we'll be thin.

ON AEROBICS

Bobbing boobs and jiggling rear,
Music playing, deafening ear,
Slithering hips and shuffling feet,
Constant pounding of the beat:
Wriggle on until you're trim . . .
. . . Then start up on some other whim.

Tomorrow! The resolution doth resound,
I'll start that diet, lose that pound;
This time, I'll make it! I won't slip!
(But first . . . One more potato chip.)

ON CATS

The feline are a fussy lot—
Psychic, too, I think;
They sit upon the very spot
Where you had thunk to sink.
When reaching for a proffered sweet,
The well-intentioned guest
Will hasten, grab a hasty treat,
Ere kitty claim the rest.
If with cat folk you'd associate,
A word to the wise, 'tis clear:
If the puss you don't ingratiate,
You'll not be welcome here!

ON KEEPING A JOURNAL

Keeping a journal's a miserable chore,
One I have often attempted before . . .

. . . with less than success

THE CREATURES IN MY ROOM ONE NIGHT

One night, as I lay tucked in bed,
A storm cloud gathered overhead,
And high above my ceiling board,
A thunder-boomer loudly roared.
Now, *I've* no fear of storms and such—
I like soft raindrops very much—
But through my window flashed a light
So very ghostly and so bright;
My entire room was *fully lit*
(Though I was not afraid one bit!)
I spied a creature quite quite horrid,
Tall and skinny with no forehead;
Then appeared from off my desk
A swollen, uninvited guest.
Next, there rose into the air,
A fearsome ball of blinding glare.
Enough for me, I quickly fled
Beneath the covers atop my bed.
With beating heart and trembling hand
I felt for the lamp upon the stand,
And, gath'ring up my courage full,
I felt the cord and gave a pull;
And though I still felt faint and weak,
I finally, bravely, took a peek.
Well, the creature who tall and skinny arose
Was merely the pole where I draped my clothes.
Upon my chair, I saw with a frown,
Was only my jacket of fleece and down,
And, best of all, that indoor moon
Was nothing more than my silver balloon.
Now I'm **bigger** and **never** get frightened
Of stuff like thunder and storms and lightnin'!
But . . .
if stuff should get scary or **really** bad,
I just hop in bed with my Mom and Dad!

SIMPLE THINGS

Time once there was, when, without pause, one just dropped by to say,
"Hello, there, Gal; how goes it Pal? What's new with you today?"
Well, that was fine, 'cause every time a knock came at the door,
Each messy mound I'd quickly round onto the closet floor.
All dishes sticky made way quickly into the washer dirty,
And pillows fluffed hid other stuff, till everything seemed purty.
With mighty huffs at tiny puffs of cobwebs, dust and grit,
I'd make my way in haste to say, "Hey, welcome; come and sit!"
And I'd be glad, no time I had, to hurriedly contemplate
Which mess was brewin', what needed doin', what did me consternate.
Couldn't hop around and shop the town until the coffers burst,
Grab each machine the house to clean and then, to make things worse,
Find need to polish, shine, fix feast to dine, plus set a lovely table;
Then dress quite neat from head to feet and look quite chic and able.

Thus, next time you'd pay a visit, hey—from warning please abstain;
Don't call ahead; just simple bread our friendship will sustain.
Your warmth and cheer are welcome here in fair or stormy weather;
And neither mind what others find, dear friend, we'll get together.

SINGING SAINTS

The lead soprano's a creature quite awesome;
Caressing her obligato
With drama great, while quite devoted
To maintaining her vibrato.

The tenor is her counterpart;
He will brook no static;
He vies with her, contesting clear,
In tones quite melismatic.

The modest alto, one will find,
Is quite content to add
The middle notes, just sings her part,
And hopes it's not too bad.

The basso profundo, no equal has,
He often stands alone
Aloof in tones of vibrant hue.
Anxious for golf and home.

The organist has, without a doubt
Freedom to be the proudest;
'Cause, after all is said and done,
His instrument is the loudest.

Oh what a tangled web we weave
When first we practice to deceive!
But when we've practiced quite a while,
How vastly we improve our style.
var. on Sir Walter Scott

TGI THURSDAY

The water bill is out of sight,
As is the cost of the 'lectric light;
The laundry soap exceeds the cost
Of ruined pies in oven lost.

The spiders feast in every room,
But I can't find my ceiling broom;
It could be done with paper toweling,
But waste would set my dear one howling.

The kids best tennies resemble swiss cheese,
Their denims are getting holey knees.
The tires on the car are shiny and slick;
The cost of gas may solve this quick.

The furniture has a lived-in look—
Nine-ninety-five for a paperback book;
They called again to shampoo the rugs;
I'd never disturb my live-in bugs!

The phone bill goes up every week,
And, I swear, I hardly ever speak
To anyone out of my "interLATA",
(Which I guess can't tell from my 'intralata.")

Tonight, it's Spam steaks, yesterday, stew,
And Spam and eggs for breakfast must do.
I'll scrimp and save and hoard my stash—
'Til tomorrow—TGIF—the paycheck I'll cash.

THE PREACHER

for Pastor Jon with Love

Our pastor is a gentle man;
His words our souls inspire;
He walks the path our dear Lord trod,
He sets our hearts afire.
Though he wears no beard, boasts shiny pate,
Standing 'neath the stained-glass cross,
He's the very image of Jesus to me
As he shares our every loss.
His sermons oft bring warm shared smiles,
Followed by heartfelt tears,
As he speaks of love and hope and joy
And faith to face our fears.
His fervent prayers uplift us all;
In Christ, forgives our sins;
He bids us come to God in prayer,
Says all in Him begins.
(He's very nearly perfect,
Except for one small thing:
He wears no watch, thus ne'er suspects:
Mom's oven's about to ding.)

THERE'S TOO MANY THINGS IN MY SOUP

There's too many peas on this plate;
There's too many peas on this plate;
I know there are more than I saw here before,
There's too many peas on this plate!

There's too many things in my soup;
There's too many things in my soup;
They look slimy to me, and I plainly can see,
There's too many things in my soup!

There's way too much meat on my dish;
There's way too much meat on my dish;
I ate all my lunch, and there's still a whole bunch;
There's way too much meat on my dish!

What happened to all my ice cream?
What happened to all my ice cream?
One spoonful, gee whiz! Is that all there is?
What happened to all my ice cream?

TURN YOUR FACE TOWARD THE SUNSHINE . . . . . . and YOU WILL NOT SEE THE SHADOWS

When the world is too much with you,
When the winds blow less than kind:
Lift your face toward the sunshine;
And the shadows fall behind

When you feel the dark enfold you
And dread fears caress your mind:
Look in hope up to the sunshine,
And let shadows fall behind.

When black rain clouds hover 'round you,
And tears make bright eyes blind:
Walk in faith forth to the Son Shine,
And all shadows melt behind.

T.V. SHOULD CHANGE ITS IMAGE—I CAN'T SEEM TO CHANGE MINE

With all the hype on the old T.V.,
I'm convinced I'll never competent be.
I haven't ordered a record set;
I haven't changed my toothpaste yet
To one which takes one's breath away;
I haven't done yoga yet today.
In my toilet, there's no little man,
There's ordinary old bags in my garbage can.
The teeth of our dog are noticeably yellow;
I forgot those bones for that good old fellow.
My legs have bristles from ankles to knees;
I'll get that cream later, if I please.
I quit smoking years back, however I've yet
To break myself of Nicorette.
As for the stingy peck I get each morning,
Must I really rinse first and without warning?
My reflection in my furniture I've rarely seen;
Perhaps my counters are really unclean?
I polish all day till it smells like fruit;
Seems shiny enough for the fingerprints cute.
I've held my blow dryer to my hip,
But the attitude doesn't really fit;
I'll try it with a cowboy hat;
Might get some mileage out of that.
I haven't called the exterminator this year;
Come to think of it, he's never been here.
My significant other doesn't buy fried chicken
Every Friday night for finger lickin'.
Even if I do deserve a break today,
Don't have the time to get away.
I've never had flowers from F.T.D.,
But then, all sexed up I'll never be
At four P.M., in some clinging dress,

Romantically awaiting a long caress.
When my dear one walks in, he checks out the stove;
That's about a far as his fingers rove.
Those bubble-bathing beauties seen on T.V.,
Don't they have kids? Where could they be.
No odor gulpers in the socks,
No bloody Marys on the rocks.
No flower-fresh meadows from candlesbloom,
Sweet scent eau-de-musty pervades every room
No fax machine, no speaker phone;
No voice mail answers when no one's home.
No bottom soothing toilet paper;
And it's mashed potatoes, not stuffing, later.
We surely will all expire quite soon
If all those preservatives we continue to consume.
It seems I haven't done much that's right;
I'll probably lie awake all night.
My cold pills aren't time release;
My cake, not moist in every piece.
My hose have ugly panty lines;
My face has age's tell-tale signs.

I've decided I've been remiss enough;
I vow, I'll get the proper stuff
To make my life a life of ease,
Use products guaranteed to please.
I'll haunt down every market aisle,
Persueing excellence with a smile
Of vengence, proudly, on my lips;
I did it all in just six trips.
I gathered up my whole collection
For weeks of toil and introspection.
Are now my windows ammonia bright:
Is washline hung with clothes pure white?
Does my morning breath smell now much sweeter:
Is my whole house entirely neater?
Are now my legs quite soft and smoothe?
Above all . . .

Am I the victim of some ad man's ruse?
I guess there's no one but me to blame,
But, strangely, everythings still the same.
I've gone back to my former ways,
Wand'ring through a familiar haze.
One small souvignier of my folly—parlysis
But my lip is still hairless, thanks to "pain-free" electrolosis.

TWINKLE, TWINKLE YOU'RE MY STAR

for Nick

Twinkle, twinkle, little star,
How I wonder what you are!

Would you come and play with me,
Shining here for all to see?

You and I, we'll gaily fly,
Gliding through the nighttime sky.

With the other stars we'll play
All along the Milky Way;

Spin and twirl and very soon
Slide on down to Mr. Moon.

He greets us with his friendly smile
And rests us on his lap a while.

He'll gently rock us to and fro,
As we peek down on earth below.

But, oh, see there, Miss Sun's first ray
Comes to chase the night away.

My star grows dim; he has to go.
But, when I look up from earth below

On any moonlit, starry night,
He promised me he'll twinkle bright;

On me he'll always gently beam,
And send me pleasant, happy dreams.

All I'll ever have to do
Is wish on him, and dreams come true.

Twinkle, twinkle little star . . .
My special friend is what you are!

BOATERS

Types of boaters, there are two;
Each of these is known to you:
The gentleman sailor rides the lake,
Avoiding the hotdog's roaring wake.

The bonafide sailor skims the lake
In leisure manner, sail doth take.
He joins the yacht club and regatta,
Just the way a gentleman ought-ta.
But the demon who drives with roaring motor
Is much the lesser breed of boater;
Shall the sailor pretend he hath not heard,
Or, deliver his sentiments via "the bird"?

THE VERY BAD DAY

I'm just so mad,
How could I be glad,
After the rat-rotten day that I've had.
I awoke with a scream
From the fearsomest dream,.
As you would, too, if that monster you'd seen!
Out side was still dark;
But I heard a dog bark
In the light of the moon by the tree in the park.
I crawled down in bed
And covered my head,
When I heard my mom holler: "Get up now!" she said.
She called out, "You're late!
And the eggs on your plate
Are already cold, and the bus comes at eight!"
Though I wet down my hair;
It still stuck in the air,
So I spit on my hand and I plastered it there.
My one sock was blue;
Now what should I do?
Where the matching one was, I hadn't a clue!
I grabbed my high tops
Which covered my socks,
So no one would see one was red as a fox.
As I gulped down my food,
I choked as I chewed,
And Mom said, "Now stop that! You're being quite rude!"
Then Mom gave me a hug,
And I tripped on the rug;
My sister whooped, "Man, you're a clumsy big lug!"
Turned to wave at my pop,
Tripped over a rock
And tore my new pants on the bumpity walk.
For a time, all went well;
I made school by the bell,
But what happened next, it grieves me to tell!

I pulled out my math
And heard all my pals laugh;
It seems, when I fell, all my books took a bath.
Teacher was vexed,
And I was perplexed
Then I lost out on spelling the simple word "next".
Hot doggies! It's noon!
And lunchtime is soon;
Nothing can fill that brief respite with gloom!
Oh, No? How 'bout this:
Not one fellow did miss
When yucky Jane Clucky gave me a big kiss!
Well, they laughed and they teased,
And they called me diseased;
When that recess was over, I surely was pleased.
Now it's gym; I just hope
They don't call me a dope
Just cuz last time I fell while climbing the rope.
Oh, no; won't this stop?
I just spilled my red pop
All over my teacher, and way more than a drop!
Hooray! Clock strikes three;
And I'm finally free
To go home all alone, and be only with me.
Well, I made it through dinner;
Perhaps there's a glimmer
Of making it up and to bed like a winner.
I'll just slip on upstairs,
Where nobody cares,
Kneel down on scraped knees and say all of my prayers.
Heav'n's stars twinkle bright
As I close my eyes tight,
And my folks tiptoe in, kiss me softly good night.

I curl into a ball,
All cozy and small,

And surmise it was not a bad day after all.

WILL SOMEONE PLEASE ANSWER THE RING IN THE TUB?

Ever longed to take a soak
In blessed solitude,
To slip beneath those bubbles warm
All comfy, cozy, nude.
Really live it up—champagne,
Soft candle scent, a book?
Semi-retired in perfect bliss;
No thoughts of clean or cook?
Drift off and just forget the chores,
The kids, the hockey, the rides;
Float therein and contemplate
You navel, knees, and sides
Don't you love it? Ain't it grand
To luxuriate in peace?
Well, hold on to that thought, my friend,
No doubt it soon will cease!
Yep, here we go; they're at it again;
The boys are in a fight:
"Those socks are mine, one brown one blue,
One tube-top and one white"
"Ma," the other hollers loud,
"Stupid's got my sock!"
"I haven't either," the first yells back,
"I'll knock him in the block!"
"I had two rights to my blue pair,
And he has extra red."
"I need the extra right." says he,
"To make my mouse a bed."
"What are you doing in my room?"
This shout comes from the sister.
"If you've been reading my diary again,
You'd best start praying, mister!"
"I only need a sock," says he;
"I could use some panty hose."

"Oh, no, you don't, you keep your mouse
In someone else's clother."
All at once, it's silent, still;
I'd really better hurry;
Whenever there's no noise at all,
There's reason good to worry.
Out of the tub, into the robe,
Champagne glass hits the floor;
No time for dusting powder now,
I bolt out through the door.
There stand three little cherubs,
Sweet smiles upon each face;
A fearsome thing for a mom to see;
But all seems quite in place.
She looks around, just one more glance,
Well, everything seems better;
Until she sees, all cuddled up,
A mouse in her cashmere sweater.

THE WRIGGLY, SQUIGGLY WORM

for Zack

At night, the wriggly, squiggly worm
Slides out and slithers 'round,
But in the morn, when robins come,
He slips back in the ground.

What does he do all day, this slug,
So far from light and sky?
Does he have friends with whom to play,
The same as you and I?

Whatever, he must happy be;
He never needs a mate.
He merely smiles at his other end
And shyly makes a date.

THE WRITER

As a writer, I must say,
I sure don't do it every day,
Though constant blurbs of endless rhyme
palpitate in constant time.
A nobler phrase I've never written,
than that, "I gets antsy when I'm sittin."

Edwards Brothers Malloy
Thorofare, NJ USA
November 27, 2012